The Usborne Book of Christmas Poems

Designers: Mary Cartwright, Michelle Lawrence,
Hanri Van Wyck and Katie Lovell

The Usborne Book of Christmas Poems

Collected by Sam Taplin

Illustrated by Anna Luraschi

When I hear the word Christmas, I think of the staircase in the house where I grew up. On Christmas Day, I would dash downstairs as fast as I could, knowing I was about to step not into our living room but into an extraordinary place with presents scattered on the floor and magic in the air. Today, when I hear the first notes of a familiar carol or sit by the fire on Christmas Eve, I feel the same sense of excitement that used to rush through me as I sprinted down those steps.

I think poems are a great way to capture the spirit of Christmas. There's something about a poem, with its enchanting rhythms and beautiful images, that makes it especially good at expressing the magic of it all. In this book, I've tried to include verses which reflect all the different moods of the season…a baby in a manger, Santa soaring through the night sky, the stress of writing "thank you" letters – it's all here. Whatever Christmas means to you, I hope you enjoy the poems.

Sam Taplin, Oxford, 2005

Contents

A Visit from St. Nicholas

'Twas the night before Christmas,
when all through the house
Not a creature was stirring, not even a mouse;
The stockings were hung by the chimney with care,
In hopes that St. Nicholas soon would be there;
The children were nestled all snug in their beds,
While visions of sugar-plums danced in their heads;
And mamma in her 'kerchief, and I in my cap,
Had just settled our brains for a long winter's nap,

When out on the lawn there arose such a clatter,
I sprang from the bed to see what was the matter.
Away to the window I flew like a flash,
Tore open the shutters and threw up the sash.
The moon on the breast of the new-fallen snow
Gave the lustre of mid-day to objects below,
When, what to my wondering eyes should appear,
But a miniature sleigh, and eight tiny reindeer,

With a little old driver, so lively and quick,
I knew in a moment it must be St. Nick.
More rapid than eagles his coursers they came,
And he whistled, and shouted,
And called them by name;
"Now, Dasher! now, Dancer!
Now, Prancer and Vixen!
On, Comet! on Cupid!
On, Donner and Blitzen!
To the top of the porch!
To the top of the wall!
Now dash away!
Dash away! dash away all!"

As dry leaves that before the wild hurricane fly,
When they meet with an obstacle, mount to the sky,
So up to the house-top the coursers they flew,
With the sleigh full of toys, and St. Nicholas too.
And then, in a twinkling, I heard on the roof
The prancing and pawing of each little hoof.
As I drew in my head, and was turning around,
Down the chimney St. Nicholas came with a bound.

He was dressed all in fur,
From his head to his foot,
And his clothes were all
Tarnished with ashes and soot;
A bundle of toys he had
Flung on his back,
And he looked like a pedlar
Just opening his pack.

His eyes – how they twinkled!
His dimples, how merry!
His cheeks were like roses, his nose like a cherry!
His droll little mouth was drawn up like a bow,
And the beard of his chin was as white as the snow;
The stump of a pipe he held tight in his teeth,
And the smoke it encircled his head like a wreath;
He had a broad face and a little round belly,
That shook when he laughed like a bowlful of jelly.
He was chubby and plump, a right jolly old elf,

And I laughed when I saw him,
In spite of myself;
A wink of his eye
And a twist of his head,
Soon gave me to know
I had nothing to dread.
He spoke not a word,
But went straight to his work,
And filled all the stockings; then turned with a jerk,
And laying his finger aside of his nose,
And giving a nod, up the chimney he rose;
He sprang to his sleigh, to his team gave a whistle,
And away they all flew like the down of a thistle.
But I heard him exclaim, 'ere he drove out of sight,

"Merry Christmas to all,
        and to all a goodnight."

Clement Clarke Moore

Christmas Thank yous

Dear Auntie
Oh, what a nice jumper
I've always adored powder blue
and fancy you thinking of
orange and pink
for the stripes
how clever of you!

14

Dear Uncle
The soap is
terrific
So
useful
and such a kind thought and
how did you guess that
I'd just used the last of
the soap that last Christmas brought

Dear Gran
Many thanks for the hankies
Now I really can't wait for the flu
and the daisies embroidered
in red round the "M"
for Michael
how
thoughtful of you!

Dear Cousin
What socks!
and the same sort you wear
so you must be
the last word in style
and I'm certain you're right that the
luminous green
will make me stand out a mile

16

Dear Sister
I quite understand your concern
it's a risk sending jam in the post
But I think I've pulled out
all the big bits
of glass
so it won't taste too sharp
spread on toast

Dear Grandad
Don't fret
I'm delighted
So *don't* think your gift will
offend
I'm not at all hurt
that you gave up this year
and just sent me
a fiver
to spend

Mick Gowar

17

The Waiting Game

Nuts and marbles in the toe,
An orange in the heel,
A Christmas stocking in the dark
Is wonderful to feel.

Shadowy, bulging length of leg
That crackles when you clutch,
A Christmas stocking in the dark
Is marvellous to touch.

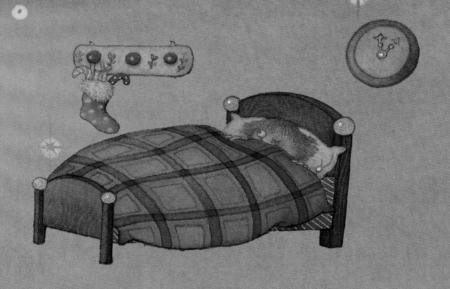

You lie back on your pillow
But that shape's still hanging there.
A Christmas stocking in the dark
Is very hard to bear.

So try to get to sleep again
And chase the hours away.
A Christmas stocking in the dark
Must wait for Christmas Day.

John Mole

Christmas Bells

I heard the bells on Christmas Day
Their old familiar carols play,
And wild and sweet
The words repeat
Of "Peace on earth, good will to men!"

And thought how, as the day had come,
The belfries of all Christendom
Had rolled along
The unbroken song
Of "Peace on earth, good will to men!"

Till ringing, singing on its way,
The world revolved from night to day —
A voice, a chime,
A chant sublime
Of "Peace on earth, good will to men!"

And in despair I bowed my head;
"There is no peace on earth," I said,
"For hate is strong,
And mocks the song
Of peace on earth, good will to men!"

Then pealed the bells more loud and deep:
"God is not dead; nor doth he sleep!
The wrong shall fail,
The right prevail,
With peace on earth, good will to men!"

Henry Wadsworth Longfellow

Nativity Play

This year…
This year can I be Herod?
This year, can I be him?
A wise man
or a Joseph?
An inn man
or a king?

This year…
can I be famous?
This year, can I be best?
Bear a crown of silver
and wear a golden vest?

This year…
can I be starlight?
This year, can I stand out?

...feel the swish of curtains
and hear the front row shout
"Hurrah" for good old Ronny
he brings a gift of gold
head afire with tinsel
"The Greatest Story Told..."
"Hurrah for good old Herod!"
and shepherds from afar.

So –
don't make me a palm tree
And can I be –
      a Star?

Peter Dixon

In the Bleak Midwinter

In the bleak midwinter
Frosty wind made moan;
Earth stood hard as iron,
Water like a stone;
Snow had fallen, snow on snow,
Snow on snow,
In the bleak midwinter,
Long ago.

Our God, heaven cannot hold Him,
Nor earth sustain;
Heaven and earth shall flee away
When He comes to reign;
In the bleak midwinter
A stable-place sufficed
The Lord God almighty,
Jesus Christ.

Enough for Him whom cherubim
Worship night and day,
A breastful of milk
And a mangerful of hay;
Enough for Him whom angels
Fall down before,
The ox and ass and camel
Which adore.

Angels and archangels
May have gathered there,
Cherubim and seraphim
Thronged the air;
But only His mother
In her maiden bliss
Worshipped the Beloved
With a kiss.

What can I give Him,
Poor as I am?
If I were a shepherd
I would bring a lamb;
If I were a wise man
I would do my part;
Yet what I can, I give Him,
Give my heart.

Christina Rossetti

Talking Turkeys

Be nice to yu turkeys dis christmas
Cos turkeys jus wanna hav fun
Turkeys are cool, turkeys are wicked
An every turkey has a Mum.
Be nice to yu turkeys dis christmas,
Don't eat it, keep it alive,
It could be yu mate, an not on yu plate
Say, Yo! Turkey I'm on your side.

I got lots of friends who are turkeys
An all of dem fear christmas time,
Dey wanna enjoy it, dey say humans destroyed it
An humans are out of dere mind,
Yeah, I got lots of friends who are turkeys
Dey all hav a right to a life,
Not to be caged up an genetically made up
By any farmer an his wife.

Turkeys jus wanna play reggae
Turkeys jus wanna hip-hop
Can yu imagine a nice young turkey saying,
"I cannot wait for de chop"?
Turkeys like getting presents, dey wanna
watch christmas TV,
Turkeys hav brains an turkeys feel pain
In many ways like yu an me.

I once knew a turkey called Turkey
He said "Benji explain to me please,
Who put de turkey in christmas
An what happens to christmas trees?"
I said "I am not too sure turkey
But it's nothing to do wid Christ Mass
Humans get greedy an waste more dan need be
An business men mek loadsa cash."

Be nice to yu turkey dis christmas
Invite dem indoors fe sum greens
Let dem eat cake an let dem partake
In a plate of organic grown beans,
Be nice to yu turkey dis christmas
An spare dem de cut of de knife,
Join Turkeys United an dey'll be delighted
An yu will mek new friends FOR LIFE.

Benjamin Zephaniah

Santa Claus

I won't go to sleep

Fur coat, fur hat, and fur-lined gloves,
And now he pulls his snowboots on.
His sledge is piled with sacks and sacks:
I'll wish again before it's gone.

I won't go to sleep

He walks the paddock deep in snow,
He harnesses his reindeer team.
The reindeer snort and shake their heads;
Their bells and harness-buckles gleam.

I WON'T go to sleep

Their comet rises through the air;
Fast-falling snowflakes pass them by.
With silent hooves and shaken bells
They stream across the starlit sky.

I…won't…go…to…

Clive Sansom

Reindeer Report

Chimneys: colder.
Flightpaths: busier.
Driver: Christmas (F)
Still baffled by postcodes.

Children: more
And stay up later.
Presents: heavier.
Pay: frozen.

Mission in spite
Of all this
Accomplished.

U.A.Fanthorpe

Kings Came Riding

Kings came riding
  One, two, and three,
Over the desert
  And over the sea.

One in a ship
  With a silver mast;
The fishermen wondered
  As he went past.

One on a horse
  With a saddle of gold;
The children came running
  To behold.

One came walking,
    Over the sand,
With a casket of treasure
    Held in his hand.

All the people
    Said, "Where go they?"
But the kings went forward
    All through the day.

Night came on
    As those kings went by;
They shone like the gleaming
    Stars in the sky.

Charles Williams

Christmas in the Doghouse

It was Christmas day in the doghouse,
and no one had a bone,
and one dog who was desperate
was chewing up the phone-book,
when suddenly to their surprise
a canine Santa came
and luckily they had no logs
or he'd have been aflame.

Good news I bring the Santa said
('cos he knew how to speak)
from now on I'll be visiting the doghouse
once a week,
we'll break the human habit
they seem to hold so dear;
good will to fellow creatures,
but only once a year.

It's true we tend to urinate
around the Christmas tree,
but we're fit to lead
and not be led
in spreading Christmas glee.

They didn't want a sermon though
that's not why he was there
they all piled in like vermin
to his sack of Christmas fare,
and they eated all the bones up
and they treated Santa rough,
and as he left the doghouse
he said once a year's enough.

John Hegley

In the Town

Joseph   Take heart, the journey's ended:
I see the twinkling lights,
Where we shall be befriended
On this the night of nights.

Mary   Now praise the Lord that led us
So safe into the town,
Where men will feed and bed us,
And I can lay me down.

Joseph	And how then shall we praise him?
	Alas, my heart is sore
	That we no gifts can raise him,
	We are so very poor.

Mary	We have as much as any
	That on the earth do live,
	For though we have no penny,
	We have ourselves to give.

Joseph	Look yonder, wife, look yonder!
	A hostelry I see,
	Where travellers that wander
	Will very welcome be.

41

Mary

The house is tall and stately,
The door stands open thus;
Yet husband, I fear greatly
That inn is not for us.

Joseph

God save you, gentle master!
Your littlest room indeed
With plainest walls of plaster
Tonight will serve our need.

Innkeeper

For lordlings and for ladies
I've lodgings and to spare;
For you and yonder maid is
No closet anywhere.

Joseph

Take heart, take heart, sweet Mary,
Another inn I spy,
Whose host will not be chary
To let us easy lie.

Mary	O aid me, I am ailing,
	My strength is nearly gone;
	I feel my limbs are failing,
	And yet we must go on.
Joseph	God save you, Hostess, kindly!
	I pray you, house my wife,
	Who bears beside me blindly
	The burden of her life.
Innkeeper's wife	My guests are rich men's daughters
	And sons, I'd have you know!
	Seek out the poorer quarters,
	Where ragged people go.

Joseph	Good sir, my wife's in labour,
	Some corner let us keep.
Innkeeper	Not I: knock up my neighbour,
	And as for me, I'll sleep.
Mary	In all the lighted city
	Where rich men welcome win,
	Will not one house for pity
	Take two poor strangers in?
Joseph	Good woman, I implore you,
	Afford my wife a bed.
Innkeeper's wife	Nay, nay, I've nothing for you
	Except the cattle shed.

Mary	Then gladly in the manger Our bodies we will house, Since men tonight are stranger Than asses are and cows.
Joseph	Take heart, take heart, sweet Mary, The cattle are our friends, Lie down, lie down, sweet Mary, For here our journey ends.
Mary	Now praise the Lord that found me This shelter in the town, Where I with friends around me May lay my burden down.
Anon	

The Great Present Muddle

Santa's in a muddle,
Santa's in a mess.
He muddled all the labels
...and father got a dress.

Mother got some football boots,
Grandad got a star,
Auntie got some roller skates
And Uncle got a bra.
My cousin wanted knickers,
but she got a big white rat.
Arthur asked for whisky
and got a silly hat.
Johnny said
"A racing bike"
but Johnny got a rose.
Grandma got a football
and Frank's designer clothes.

Oh what an awful muddle!
Which belongs to who?

I'm sure you know the answer,
so I leave it up to you.

Peter Dixon

The Oxen

Christmas Eve, and twelve of the clock.
"Now they are all on their knees,"
An elder said as we sat in a flock
By the embers in hearthside ease.

We pictured the meek mild creatures where
They dwelt in their strawy pen,
Nor did it occur to one of us there
To doubt they were kneeling then.

So fair a fancy few would weave
In these years! Yet, I feel,
If someone said on Christmas Eve,
"Come; see the oxen kneel

"In the lonely barton by yonder coomb
Our childhood used to know,"
I should go with him in the gloom,
Hoping it might be so.

Thomas Hardy

49

The Christmas Tree

They chopped her down in some far wood
A week ago,
Shook from her dark green spikes her load
Of gathered snow,
And brought her home at last, to be
Our Christmas show.

A week she shone, sprinkled with lamps
And fairy frost;
Now, with her boughs all stripped, her lights
And spangles lost,
Out in the garden there, leaning
On a broken post,

She sighs gently…Can it be
She longs to go
Back to that far-off wood, where green
And wild things grow?
Back to her dark green sisters, standing
In wind and snow?

John Walsh

A Christmas Carol

The Christ-child lay on Mary's lap,
   His hair was like a light.
(O weary, weary were the world,
   But here is all aright.)

The Christ-child lay on Mary's breast,
   His hair was like a star.
(O stern and cunning are the kings,
   But here the true hearts are.)

The Christ-child lay on Mary's heart,
   His hair was like a fire.
(O weary, weary is the world,
   But here the world's desire.)

The Christ-child stood at Mary's knee,
His hair was like a crown,
And all the flowers looked up at him,
And all the stars looked down.

G.K.Chesterton

Christmas at the Zoo

Early Christmas morning,
Christmas at the zoo,
They've all hung up their stockings —
The gorilla and the gnu,
The walrus and the crocodile,
The skunk, the kangaroo.

Let's see what Santa's brought them
To unwrap on Christmas Day —
For the chest beating gorilla
There's a bongo drum to play,
For the gnu a box of gnougat,
For the skunk, deodorant spray.

A rattle for the bushbaby,
Playing cards for the cheetah,
Belgian chocolate covered ants
For the greedy anteater,
Some scissors for the walrus
To keep his moustache neater.

Balloons for the baboons,
Toothpicks for the crocs,
Ribbons for the gibbons,
Skis for the Arctic fox,
For the octopus in the aquarium
Four pairs of woolly socks.

There's a joke book for the hyena —
Hyenas love to laugh —
A jumper for the kangaroo,
And as for the giraffe —
A very, very, very, very,
Very long scarf.

There's eye-shadow for the panda,
A brush for the mountain hare,
Sticky sweets for parakeets,
A teddy for the bear,
And for the bald-headed eagle,
A nice warm hat to wear.

Yes, early Christmas morning,
Christmas at the zoo,
They're so pleased with their presents —
The gorilla, the gnu,
The walrus and the crocodile,
The skunk, the kangaroo.

Richard Edwards

Moonless Darkness Stands Between

58

Moonless darkness stands between.
Past, O Past, no more be seen!
But the Bethlehem star may lead me
To the sight of Him who freed me
From the self that I have been.
Make me pure, Lord: Thou art holy;
Make me meek, Lord: Thou wert lowly;
Now beginning, and alway:
Now begin, on Christmas day.

Gerard Manley Hopkins

Minstrels

The minstrels played their Christmas tune
Tonight beneath my cottage-eaves;
While, smitten by a lofty moon,
The encircling laurels, thick with leaves,
Gave back a rich and dazzling sheen,
That overpowered their natural green.

Through hill and valley every breeze
Had sunk to rest with folded wings:
Keen was the air, but could not freeze,
Nor check, the music of the strings;
So stout and hardy were the band
That scraped the chords with strenuous hand.

And who but listened? – till was paid
Respect to every inmate's claim,
The greeting given, the music played
In honour of each household name,
Duly pronounced with lusty call,
And "Merry Christmas" wished to all.

William Wordsworth

They're Fetching in Ivy and Holly

"They're fetching in ivy and holly
And putting it this way and that.
I simply can't think of the reason,"
Said Si-Si the Siamese cat.

"They're pinning up lanterns and streamers.
There's mistletoe over the door.
They've brought in a tree from the garden.
I do wish I knew what it's for.

"It's covered with little glass candles
That go on and off without stop.
They've put it to stand in a corner
And tied up a fairy on top.

"They're stringing bright cards by the dozen
And letting them hang in a row.
Some people outside in the roadway
Are singing a song in the snow.

"I saw all the children write letters
And – I'm not at all sure this was wise –
They posted each one *up the chimney*.
I couldn't believe my own eyes.

"What on earth, in the middle of winter,
Does the family think it is at?
Won't somebody please come and tell me?"
Said Si-Si the Siamese cat.

Charles Causley

little tree

little tree
little silent Christmas tree
you are so little
you are more like a flower

who found you in the green forest
and were you very sorry to come away?
see   i will comfort you
because you smell so sweetly

i will kiss your cool bark
and hug you safe and tight
just as your mother would,
only don't be afraid

look   the spangles
that sleep all the year in a dark box
dreaming of being taken out and allowed to shine,
the balls the chains red and gold the fluffy threads,

put up your little arms
and i'll give them all to you to hold
every finger shall have its ring
and there won't be a single place dark or unhappy

then when you're quite dressed
you'll stand in the window for everyone to see
and how they'll stare!
oh but you'll be very proud

and my little sister and i will take hands
and looking up at our beautiful tree
we'll dance and sing
"Noel Noel"

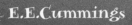
E.E.Cummings

This Christmas

This Christmas I won't buy a tree,
I'll stretch my arms instead,
And stand up in the window
With a fairy on my head,
With tinsel wrapped all round me
From my shoulders to my toes,
And presents piled up to my knees,
And glitter on my nose.

Richard Edwards

December

Glad Christmas comes, and every hearth
Makes room to give him welcome now,
E'en want will dry its tears in mirth,
And crown him with a holly bough;
Though tramping 'neath a winter sky,
O'er snowy paths and rimy stiles,
The housewife sets her spinning by
To bid him welcome with her smiles.

Each house is swept the day before,
And windows stuck with evergreens,
The snow is besom'd from the door,
And comfort crowns the cottage scenes.
Gilt holly, with its thorny pricks,
And yew and box, with berries small,
These deck the unused candlesticks,
And pictures hanging by the wall.

Neighbours resume their annual cheer,
Wishing, with smiles and spirits high,
Glad Christmas and a happy year
To every morning passer-by;
Milkmaids their Christmas journeys go,
Accompanied with favour'd swain;
And children pace the crumping snow,
To taste their granny's cake again.

The shepherd, now no more afraid,
Since custom doth the chance bestow,
Starts up to kiss the giggling maid
Beneath the branch of mistletoe
That 'neath each cottage beam is seen,
With pearl-like berries shining gay;
The shadow still of what hath been,
Which fashion yearly fades away.

John Clare

Pudding Charms

Our Christmas pudding was made in November,
All they put in it, I quite well remember:
Currants and raisins, and sugar and spice,
Orange peel, lemon peel – everything nice
Mixed up together, and put in a pan.
"When you've stirred it," said Mother, "as much as you can,
We'll cover it over, that nothing may spoil it,
And then, in the copper, tomorrow we'll boil it."
That night, when we children were all fast asleep,
A real fairy godmother came crip-a-creep!

She wore a red cloak, and a tall steeple hat
(Though nobody saw her but Tinker, the cat!)
And out of her pocket a thimble she drew,
A button of silver, a silver horse-shoe,
And, whisp'ring a charm in the pudding pan popped them,
Then flew up the chimney directly she dropped them;
And even old Tinker pretended he slept
(With Tinker a secret is sure to be kept!),
So nobody knew, until Christmas came round,
And there, in the pudding, these treasures were found.

Charlotte Druitt Cole

Santa's New Idea

Said Santa Claus
One winter's night,
"I really think it's only right
That gifts should have a little say
'Bout where they'll be on Christmas Day."

So then and there
He called the toys
Intended for good girls and boys,
And when they'd settled down to hear,
He made his plan for them quite clear.

These were his words:
"Soon now," said he,
"You'll all be speeding off with me
To bring the Christmas joy and cheer
To little ones both far and near.

"Here's my idea,
It seems but fair
That you should each one have a share
In choosing homes where you will stay
On and after Christmas Day.

"During the next weeks
Before we go
Over the miles of glistening snow
Find out the tots you like the best
And think much nicer than the rest."

The toys called out
"Hurrah! Hurray!
What fun to live always and play
With folks we choose – they'll surely be
Selected very carefully."

So, children dear,
When you do see
Your toys in socks or on a tree,
You'll know in all the world 'twas you
They wanted to be given to.

Anon

Before the Paling of the Stars

Before the paling of the stars,
Before the winter morn,
Before the earliest cock-crow,
Jesus Christ was born:
Born in a stable,
Cradled in a manger,
In the world His hands had made
Born a stranger.

Priest and King lay fast asleep
In Jerusalem;
Young and old lay fast asleep
In crowded Bethlehem;
Saint and Angel, ox and ass,
Kept a watch together,
Before the Christmas daybreak
In the winter weather.

Jesus on His Mother's breast
In the stable cold,
Spotless Lamb of God was he,
Shepherd of the fold:
Let us kneel with Mary Maid,
With Joseph bent and hoary,
With Saint and Angel, ox and ass,
To hail the King of Glory.

Christina Rossetti

The Christmas Life

If you don't have a real tree, you don't bring the Christmas life into the house.

Josephine Mackinnon, aged 8

Bring in a tree, a young Norwegian spruce,
Bring hyacinths that rooted in the cold,
Bring winter jasmine as its buds unfold:
Bring the Christmas life into this house.

Bring red and green and gold, bring things that shine,
Bring candlesticks and music, food and wine.
Bring in your memories of Christmas past,
Bring in your tears for all that you have lost.

Bring in the shepherd boy, the ox and ass,
Bring in the stillness of an icy night,
Bring in a birth, of hope and love and light:
Bring the Christmas life into this house.

Wendy Cope

The Old Year

The Old Year's gone away
To nothingness and night:
We cannot find him all the day
Nor hear him in the night:
He left no footstep, mark or place
In either shade or sun:
The last year he'd a neighbour's face,
In this he's known by none.

All nothing everywhere:
Mists we on mornings see
Have more of substance when they're here
And more of form than he.
He was a friend by every fire,
In every cot and hall –
A guest to every heart's desire,
And now he's nought at all.

Old papers thrown away,
Old garments cast aside,
The talk of yesterday,
All things identified;
But times once torn away
No voices can recall:
The eve of New Year's Day
Left the Old Year lost to all.

John Clare

from In Memoriam

Ring out, wild bells, to the wild sky,
The flying cloud, the frosty light:
The year is dying in the night;
Ring out, wild bells, and let him die.

Ring out the old, ring in the new,
Ring, happy bells, across the snow:
The year is going, let him go;
Ring out the false, ring in the true.

Ring out the grief that saps the mind,
For those that here we see no more;
Ring out the feud of rich and poor,
Ring in redress to all mankind.

Ring out a slowly dying cause,
And ancient forms of party strife;
Ring in the nobler modes of life,
With sweeter manners, purer laws.

Ring out the want, the care, the sin,
The faithless coldness of the times;
Ring out, ring out my mournful rhymes,
But ring the fuller minstrel in.

Ring out false pride in place and blood,
The civic slander and the spite;
Ring in the love of truth and right,
Ring in the common love of good.

Ring out old shapes of foul disease;
Ring out the narrowing lust of gold;
Ring out the thousand years of old,
Ring in the thousand years of peace.

Ring in the valiant man and free,
The larger heart, the kindlier hand;
Ring out the darkness of the land,
Ring in the Christ that is to be.

Alfred Tennyson

87

The New Year

Here we bring new water
From the well so clear,
For to worship God with,
This happy New Year.
Sing levy-dew, sing levy-dew,
The water and the wine;
The seven bright gold wires
And the bugles they do shine.

Sing reign of Fair Maid,
With gold upon her toe –
Open you the West Door,
And turn the Old Year go:
Sing reign of Fair Maid,
With gold upon her chin –
Open you the East Door,
And let the New Year in.

Anon

Christmas Poem Competition

It's the night before Christmas, the year's at an end,
And our poems have asked to be sent a new friend.
And so we would like you to write something new,
A verse that describes what the day means to you.
You can write about Santa, the presents he brings,
Or shepherds and stables and starlight and kings,

Or anything Christmassy – tinsel and snow…
Then send it to us. (See the website below.)
We'll enter your poem in our competition,
And if it's the winner, then our new edition
Of this book next Christmas will fill you with cheer:
Your poem will be on this page, printed here.
So write us a poem, there's only one rule:
Make it better than this one. Good luck – Happy Yule!

Sam Taplin

For details of how to enter the
competition, go to www.usborne.com
and click on "Write a Christmas Poem".

Index of First Lines

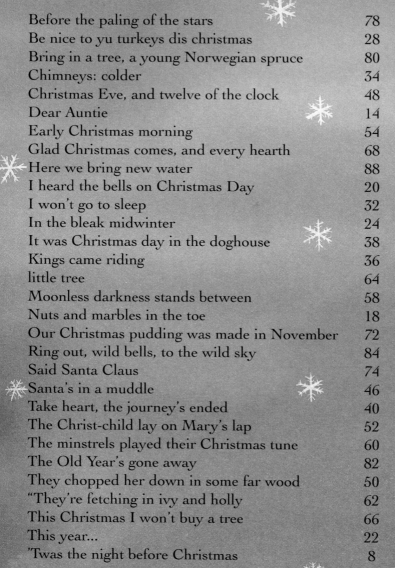

Index of Poets

Acknowledgements

Every effort has been made to trace the copyright holders of the material in this book. If any rights have been omitted, the publishers offer to rectify this in any subsequent editions following notification. The publishers are grateful to the following individuals and organizations for their permission to reproduce copyright material.

14 "Christmas Thank yous" by Mick Gowar. Reprinted by permission of HarperCollins Publishers Ltd. ©Mick Gowar.

18 "The Waiting Game" by John Mole. Reprinted by permission of John Mole. ©John Mole.

22 "Nativity Play" by Peter Dixon. Reprinted by permission of Peter Dixon. ©Peter Dixon.

28 "Talking Turkeys" by Benjamin Zephaniah. Reprinted by permission of Penguin Books Ltd. ©Benjamin Zephaniah, 1994.

32 "Santa Claus" by Clive Sansom. From *The Golden Unicorn* (Methuen). Reprinted by permission of David Higham Associates.

34 "Reindeer Report" by U.A.Fanthorpe. Reprinted by permission of Peterloo Poets. ©U.A.Fanthorpe *Collected Poems* (2005).

36 "Kings Came Riding" by Charles Williams. From *Modern Verse for Little Children*. Reprinted by permission of David Higham Associates.

38 "Christmas in the Doghouse" by John Hegley. Reprinted by permission of PFD on behalf of: John Hegley. ©John Hegley, 1991.